I Survived Through God's Grace and Mercy

My Life Story an Autobiography

By
Nadine Bennett

Printed in the United States of America.

All Scriptures are taken from the King James Version of the Bible.

First Printing, 2018

ISBN: 13: 978-1987408171

Author: Nadine Bennett

Published by:
ARD Book Services
www.ardbookservices.com
Hillside, IL 60026

Publishing Company

TABLE OF CONTENTS

ACKNOWLEDGEMENT

First, I want to thank God for being the head of my life. He has allowed me to tell my life story while giving me the wisdom to do it. I give unto him all the praises, all the honor and glory because my testimony and this autobiography is to glorify him and not me. Hallelujah!

INTRODUCTION

My Life Story

By Nadine Bennett

My Story is about the storms of life and all the trials and tribulations I have been through. There were happy times, sad times, hurtful moments and long terms of emotional hurts. However, I survived through God **Grace** and **Mercy.** He brought me out of them all. I do not look like what I have been through because I am still standing. Without God, I could not have done it alone. He is my Rock.

My Story has a **Beginning, Middle** and a **Now.** I believe this book is a part of a healing process that God has lead me to do. God is doing a deep cleansing from within my very soul and is releasing all that needs emptying out of me from the roots of my soul. All hidden deep scars that I had buried down through the years are now coming to the surface. All these years I was trying to escape, the pain without working out the solution but this book is helping me work it all out of me. You will be amazed what all-still lies within your soul from childhood to adult years. This is what I call the **Now** phase of my life. When you begin to get a relationship with God, he will show you who you are and all things to come.

Isaiah 43:19. "Behold I will do a new thing; now it shall spring forth; shall ye not know it, I will even make a way in the wilderness, and rivers in the desert."

My desire is to share my testimony with the world so God can get the Glory. Someone out there may be going through the same situation I have experienced but I survived. I can honestly say I am a witness for God. He brought me out and he will do the same thing for you. He is no respecter God. God is a healer, a deliverer and has healed me in many areas in my life. I am still striving for perfection in him but I can testify that God is a healer.

Thank you Heavenly Father I know who and whose I am in you today. I am who you say I am and not what man says or what man thinks of me. I speak the truth; God loves the truth and the light. I am the light of the world. I am no longer in darkness, nor am I in a box. Neither will I let people place me where they think I should be in life. No, not any more. God has delivered me and I now know who I am in Christ. God created me as his queen and in his image and this is why I can testify and say, "I Love Me."

I wrote this book because I am an Overcomer. I confess that struggles come in all shapes sizes, and colors. Fears, addictions, persecutions and worries can all seem to take over our thoughts. God tells us that we should not lose hope! Be encourage God called you an overcomer.

1 John 4:4 – Ye are of God little children, and have overcome them; because greater is he that is in you than he that is in the world.

The solution to all trials and tribulations that life takes us through is to hold on to God unchanging hands. This is what I had to do during my life's journey. Stand still and stay strong, pray and read His word and be patient. Wait on the Lord and see his salvation which he will show you over and repeatedly.

Romans 5:3-5 (3) And not only so be we glory in tribulations also; knowing that tribulation worketh patience. (4) And patience, experience and experience hope. (5) And hope maketh not ashamed, because the love of God is shed abroad, in our hearts by the Holy Ghost, which is, giveth unto us.

In Christ, it is not all about you but as a Christian, we are to be helpers to one another. In this book, you will see just how much God is Love. I am so thankful He is not through with me yet!

1 THE FIRST YEARS OF MY LIFE

I was born in Indianola, Mississippi, on June 3, 1956. I was the first born at that particular time. My parents were Mr. Charles Thomas (C.T.) and Mrs. Perthine Jackson. As I became old enough to go to school, I attended Carver Elementary. Going into the first grade, at that time, back in the nineteen sixties, you began school at the age of six. The school was about three blocks from my home. My cousins did not live very far so they would pick me up and take me to school with them. My cousins were a few years older and were used to going to school. They made me feel comfortable and took up for me if anything bad ever happened. So I really felt like I had older sisters and brothers there with me at school. I can remember the very first house we lived in on Cox Street. It was a two room wooded house sitting upon four bricks. After school, me and my cousins would joke and laugh while sitting on the big wooded porch and even sometimes watch TV. We would visit the corner candy store where I would buy my mother ginger snap cookies. My mom loved ginger snap cookies. I remember I was going to the store to get my mother a bag of cookies, and before I made it home all the cookies had spilled out of the bag leaving a long trail. I did not know that the cookies had fallen out of the bag. When I got home, my mother wanted to know where the rest of the cookies were. Therefore, she sent me back to the store to find out what happened to the cookies. As I was on my way back to the store, they were laying on the ground in a trail. I did not noticed I dropped the cookies but sure enough, they were all on the ground. I was only about 4 or 5 when this happened. This memory brings me much laughter. This is just a small history of my childhood growing up in Indianola, Mississippi.

2 MY DEVOTED MOTHER

My mother Perthine was an honorable homemaker. Altogether, my mother had 10 children... She loved her children and took very good care of all of us. My mother cleaned the house and cooked for us every day and she loved to iron our clothes. I can recall my mother washing our clothes in an aluminum tub. Back in those days, washing laundry was a lot of hard work. It was not like it is now where you can put a load of clothes in the washing machine and have the machine do all the work for you. My mom had to kneel on her knees and use a washboard or scrub board to clean and wash our family's clothes. Back in those days, you called the washing machine either a washboard or a scrub board. Then she would have to take the time to refill the tub with water to rinse the clothes. After that, she would then hang the clothes outside on a clothesline to dry. My mother was very devoted to her children. She was a beautiful person. My mom was home bound. She worked in the house and if she had to go out it would be to the grocery store or to church. Occasionally she would visit family members and would take me and my siblings Glenn, Glender, Deborah, and Christine to visit our grandmother Johnnie Mae. On weekends, my mother helped Johnnie Mae work in her café and we all ate there.

I can remember on one Easter Sunday my mother had taken us to church.. The church was a big white wooden church favoring a house. The church had an Easter egg hunt out in front of the yard. I found many eggs. My siblings did not find any so I had to share with them. Glen and Glender were twins and they were premature. I and the twins were only eleven months apart. My mother had four babies by that time. My mom was always busy with her babies, her hands were full, but with God's grace and mercy, she survived.

3 FRIGHTENED AND CONFUSED

My Father Charles was a painter and he worked hard to support the family. He worked many hours a week and found time to take me places with him. I loved to hang out with my Dad as long as he was sober. My Dad had some drinking issues and could not control his alcohol. When he did not drink too much, he was a beautiful person inward and outward. When he had nothing to drink, he was a very different person. When he was intoxicated, he was very physically abusive to my mother. I was unclear of the reason what caused him to react that way towards her. I was so fearful of my dad's action when he were in that state of mind. I did not want to be in his presence. When I see him coming staggering I will get so nervous I will sometime begin to vomit and just start to shake all over. My body was so frightened and confused.

I hardly stayed with my mother, mostly l stayed with my grandmother because of being afraid of him. When I was with my mother when the quarrel began my mother will tell me to go and get my grandma Christine to rescue her. Sometime it will be at night when there was no street light. Very seldom did you find streetlights in Mississippi at night. I would run as fast as I could to go get my grandmother who lived maybe ten minutes away from us. The abuse that I witnessed with my mother and all the suffering she went through had such a fearful impact on my childhood life. Throughout my adult years fear paralyze me for many years. I became so bashful and nervous that. I was afraid to challenge different things in life. The Spiritual teaching God taught me through the Holy Spirit is that fear is not of God

2 Timothy 1:7, "God hath not given us the spirit of fear: but of power, and of love, and of a sound mind."

Fear is false evidence appearing real!

F=False
E=Evidence
A=Appearing
R=Real

4 ESCAPE TO FREEDEOM

My mother had her sixth child in 1963 right before we left Indianola. My mother left the child with Uncle, Booker and his wife Francis Lee (who we all called Aunt T), until my mother was able to get settled in Chicago. Uncle Booker was my mother's mother Christine oldest brother. They did not have any children of their own. Aunt T had a passion for children and always helped her neighbors in the community with their children. Aunt T were a sweet heart and that is exactly what uncle Booker called his wife Sweet heart and she called uncle Booker Honey. An amazing lovely couple. Aunt T was a friendly heavy set red skin toned woman who kept a beautiful smile on her face. When she laughed, she shook all over and had a mouth full of gold teeth. Uncle Booker and Aunt T both lived to see their nineties.

My mother had about all she could take and decided to leave my father. We began to pack up our belongings to leave Mississippi. I had clothes at my grandmother Johnnie Mae house as we were heading out of the State of Mississippi so we stop by there to get the rest of my clothes. My mother sent me into the house to tell my grandmother that I needed my clothes for school. She did not want her to know we were leaving out of concern that this was my father's mother.

I was a very obedient and smart young girl back then and I always believed I had an old soul at a very young age. As I returned to the car, our cousin Phillip who were driving us to Chicago began traveling north. This all happened in the year of Nineteen Sixty Three (1963). This is how we escaped my father.

We arrived in Chicago where we stayed with relatives for a while at 1532 S. Albany, right in front of Douglas Park, on Chicago West Side. My mother re-enrolled me and my siblings into Johnson School about two blocks from where we were staying. My mother would walk with us to school daily seeing us into school and picking us up from school at the end of the day. My mother finally got a job and her own apartment so we transition to our new place at 1622 S. Christiana not far from where we were staying. My mother had to transfer my siblings and me to another school district, which was George Howland School on Sixteenth Street. I can remember my very first teacher there her name were Ms. Hopkins. Therefore, we stayed at this school and settled in. Both of our grandmothers would send boxes of new school clothing to help my mother. We had cloths for all occasions. The clothes would have nametags on them so my mom will know which piece of clothing belongs to whom. We were blessed with two lovely supportive grandparents.

Howland School had an after school program called social center. There were several games and hobbies to choose from such as pool, Ping-Pong, skating room, and dancing, just to name a few. There were numerous male teachers there to supervise the children to keep everyone safe and orderly.

Later my father died. I did not know whether to be sad or not; at least my thoughts were I would not have to be afraid anymore. My father's passing was a relief to me. As a child, I did not know any better; I was relieved from fear and anxiety, but at the same time, I wished my father could have been there to watch me grow into my woman hood and met his grandchildren and great grandchildren. In spite of his drinking issues, he loved his children and I loved my dad. I forgave him and his behavior just as "Christ forgave me". God has taught me to love and it starts in the home and among your family. I love all people and God loves me. God is love! John 15:12 my commandment is this "love each other as I have loved you."

Later on, my mother met my stepfather John. He was a very kind person. He helped my mother to take care of us and he provided food and brought us clothes. He worked as a roofer and he treated my siblings and me, as we were his own children. He watched us grow into our adult years and I was happy to see my mother smile once again. I colored this man father.

As I attended the sixth grade my teachers name was Mr.

Moore. He was very sharp, short, dark brown skin toned man. He were a nice teacher but with strict rules. We had to obey and follow his rules and if one student disobeyed the whole, classroom had to pay the penalty. Even if one got caught chewing gum in class he will call a hall party which means we all had to line up and go into the hall way. Each student one at a time had to bend over and get a lick on the bottom with a very thick paddle.

On our spring break, my classroom and several other sixth grade students went on a week trip to Washington D.C. The price was seventy-five dollars. I remember writing a letter to my uncle Willie Lee asking him if he can help, my mother pay for my trip and with no questions asked he sent my mother the money. There were three grey hound buses driving to take all the students to DC. We visited Maryland, Springfield, and Gettysburg. Once we made it to Washington, we all separately stayed in a hotel. The girls with the girls and the boys with the boys. In my room, my friend Barbara and I shared a room together and we were paired up during the entire trip. We visited the White house and I remember they had a blue room and different color rooms. We went to the Lincoln Memorial building, and we visited the Washington Monument. We rode to the top of this building on an elevator, which I read that it is 555 feet tall.

6 SUMMER VACATION

When we made it to my grandmother house from traveling all night, I would bathe and put on a change of clothing. She would have all the food prepared already for us to eat. When I was done eating, I would go into her front yard and swing on her swing set. I remember the swing set were white and made like a couch but out of metal, and would breathe the fresh country air. I had a bicycle that I would ride once I got there. My grandmother kept the bike in her neighbor's yard because he fixed on bikes. My grandmother Madear was a very independent woman. She worked hard daily doing home-care work (using today's term) but back in the day, you will call it a maid. When I stayed nights with Madear, she would call her boss to pick us up to take me to my other grandmother's house. I called my other grandmother "Momma", they would drop me off at Momma house, and Madear went on to work. Later in the evening at 5pm, a whistle would blow to let you know folks were getting off work. I knew it were time for Madear to be off because I would see her coming across the railroad track with her white uniform. She would always stop by and check on me. Then she would go on home. My other grandmother "Momma" lived in front of the railroad track in the heart of town where all the lively things were happening. She ran her own business, a café right in town. She survived by making a living selling food to her regular customers who would come in and out of the cafe. She sold bootleg alcohol, corn whiskey, (corn whiskey were clear), seal whiskey, (seal whiskey were brown) and home brew beer. I watched it all being made and sold right there before my very eyes at "Momma" cafe.

I would see older people dancing, bumping and grinding on those dusty wood floors. Some were intoxicated fallen all over the place and sometime grandma had to put a few folk out in the streets. It could have been male or female, but my grandma feared no one. It was fun to me to watch the action. The people that lived in the country of Indianola came to town to party on weekends. The city of Indianola was like a small suburban area, which had several Cafes'. The people partied from one café to the next cafe. The church street was full of people. I would keep a jar in my hand and ask people for money. When I received a certain amount enough to go to the dollar store, I would buy a giant size-coloring book combined with trace paper to draw pictures inside. Back then, coloring books cost one dollar.

My uncle would take me to Greenville, Mississippi to visit with him and his family and I remember they had a big swimming pool. I was too afraid of the water so I would just stand and look in the shallow water. My cousin knew I was afraid of the water so she would pull me in the middle of the pool to get a laugh. After playing around the pool, we would go for ice cream and then back to my grandma (Momma) house who lived across the railroad tracks. There was also an icehouse nearby where Momma would purchase ice to make her homemade ice cream. Her ice cream would always taste so good! Not to mention the bakery across the street. They sold the best glaze donuts and around the corner was an old drug store with wood floors that sold fountain drinks. I liked the strawberry scrumptious. They also sold an ice cream bar on a stick by the name of Cho-Cho. The chocolate ones were my favorite because it melted in my mouth as fast as I licked it.

Then one day on my summer vacation, I visited my aunt and she taught me how to bake a cake from scratch. She had chickens in her back yard in a coop where the chickens cackled; it meant they had laid eggs. I would go out into the yard to get the eggs needed, return into the house, and complete my cake. I remember making a 2-layer jelly cake, took it to my grandma "Momma" house, and shared it with the family. Momma had no problem feeding anyone who came around. She had a big heart of helping people.

As my summer vacation began to end it was time to return home and go back to school. I always looked forward to my summer vacations so that I can spend time with my family.

7 TRANSITIONING FROM ELEMENTARY SCHOOL

When my summer vacation ended and school started back in the fall of 1969, I was promoted and transferred to Hess Upper Grade Center on Douglas Blvd. This was my transition from Elementary to Junior High. Attending junior high was a new experience for me. This was a very new experience for me. What was different and new to me was how I had to change classes in between periods. In elementary school, I was accustomed to sitting in one classroom throughout the entire school day except for during lunch and recess. My homeroom teacher at that time was Mr. Holloway and he was a very nice teacher. This school had 3 buildings – a west wing, an east wing and a new addition. There was a swimming pool over in the West building where we would have swim classes once a week. On occasions, I would take a lunch break with my friends and we would walk over to Dave's Hot dog Restaurant on 12th and Homan. Dave has had the best hot dogs ever back in the day. We would also walk to Sears Roebuck and buy popcorn. They had the best popcorn in town. I continued attending Hess Upper Grade Center until I completed the 8th grade.

8 GROWING UP TOO FAST

Right after junior high school, that is when I started growing up too fast. I had a very short childhood and my grown up days started very early in life. I started to mature at an early age and my youthful years were more like adult years. At the age of twelve, I had a nice figure and my body was well developed way beyond the average twelve-year-old girl. So quite obviously, men would look at me as if I was old enough to be looked upon. I had taken my first drink of alcohol and learned how to smoke cigarettes at the age of twelve also.

Being the eldest of my siblings, I had to care for the younger ones in my family while my mother worked. Pretty much, I was raising myself. I spent most of my time alone. I had very little parental guidance other than to care for my siblings. I made my own decisions mostly and lots of wrong choicest in life caused me to be rebellious. Like most young girls my age, I thought I was all grown up and doing as I pleased.

I met Richard at a very young age and he showered me with gifts. I would sneak and see him in secret but when my mother found out she did all she could to try and prevent the relationship because of the age difference. He was a lot older than me. However, it was too late because my feelings were involved. I became pregnant at the age of fourteen and birth my first child Yolanda. My mother helped me in keeping her until I went back to high school. After having her, I became pregnant with my second child Martez at the age of nineteen. I moved into my own apartment after this childbirth. When my son Martez was only two months old, I became pregnant for the third time and had my son Terrance Lavelle. My children's father Richard moved in with me in the apartment. I let him move in because I was in love and I lacked wisdom, knowledge and understanding. I had all of my children out of wedlock by the same married man. Now Richard is my husband on this day for over thirty years.

There were some challenges throughout the marriage but it survived through God Grace and Mercy. God is still molding the both of us. I believe in my heart we were meant to be together. Although we went through some tough tests and trials, God brought us through the storms, one day at a time. God has healed the both of us and we are still going through the process of healing. We are still growing with God's wisdom, knowledge and understanding. Glory to God. *Mark 10-9 "What therefore God hath joined together let no man put asunder"*

At seven months pregnant with my third child, Richard and I were in a car accident. We were hit in the back of the car by a semi-trailer truck. The force of the impact knocked the car off the road into a field on the side of the road we were traveling on. We were thrown out of the car, which it caused me to go into labor. There were some people traveling on the highway as well and they saw the accident when it occurred and they called to get us medical help. We were taken to the hospital immediately afterwards. We were told that the people called for help because we were all unconscious at the time. I called them our guardian angels sent by God to rescue us in a time of need. Won't God Do It! God is always on time!

Psalms 46:1 "God is our refuge and strength, a very present help in trouble. Glory be to God!

Instantly, I had to have surgery because my spleen was ruptured. The doctors had to remove it, I was bleeding internally and they couldn't deliver the baby. Although the accident caused me to go into labor, they had to stop my labor to save my life. The very first hospital we were taken to was located in Jasper County Indiana. They couldn't do the surgery to remove my spleen because they did not have the medical surgical equipment needed to do the procedure. We were told the hospital was a small hospital in a small town so we were air lifted to Lafayette Indiana to Home Hospital to have my spleen removed. This hospital did a complete examination on me and found out my ankle was broken. The following week I had surgery on my ankle. I have a pin in my ankle today for over forty years to remind me of healing power of God's grace.

I stayed in the hospital nearly four weeks. Richard had a broken hip and minor cuts and bruises. He were the first to be released from the hospital. Richard loss his brother in the car accident. The staff of the hospital were very nice people and I was still in the hospital on my birthday when the hospital staff brought me a cake. We had so many of our relatives traveling to come and see us from near and far. I thank the Almighty God that we were still in our right mind and still standing strong and can share our testimony. My story is meant to be told and this is why God is getting the Glory and the praise. Without him saving me, I couldn't tell it all. Hallelujah.

Psalms 30:12 – "To the end that my glory may sing praise to thee, and not be silent, O Lord my God, I will give thanks unto thee forever."

After my foot surgery, I had to have therapy and was trained how to walk on crutches. By that time I was getting exhausted being in the hospital for nearly four weeks so I would do therapy twice daily so that I can be released early to go home. So I was released from the hospital still in a foot cast, and my grandmother Christine had come to my home when the accident occurred and stayed there to keep our children while we were in the hospital. She kept the house clean for us and washed our clothes, cooked food, and kept the children fed. Oh, my God she was such a blessing to us and the sweetest grandmother anyone would have loved and have.

When we both (Richard and I) were released from the hospital, we were helpless to one another. My youngest child was eleven months old and I was seven going on eight months pregnant so my Grandmother stayed with us until my due date. I call my baby Terrance my miracle baby because what I went through in the accident he went through also. He was born about five to six weeks after the tragedy. I was still in a foot cast and had staplers and stiches still in my stomach from the spleen surgery. I wasn't healed naturally but spiritually healed. It let me and others that believed know that God still work miracles on today. I am a living witness. My grandmother stayed with me until our baby got two months old. I can depend on my grandmother support because she loved our children and will visit regularly on pleasant trips as well. She will always comfort me and teach me good old wisdom. As it got closer to her time to go back home Richard and I was getting strength and was able to do for ourselves and the family. I will be so sad when my grandmother left our home and would cry like a baby.

10 LIVING IN A DAZE

At three months old, my son was diagnosed with Cerebral Palsy. I noticed he wouldn't drink but very little milk and wouldn't eat but small amounts of baby cereal. As he got older his condition, worsen. He couldn't swallow properly because of the damages to his brain. He couldn't grasp when his mouth was full of saliva. We had to use a suction machine to clear the saliva out of his mouth to prevent him from choking on a regular basis. Throughout each day, he wasn't growing properly. He was very small for his age and he didn't learn to talk or walk. He was also blind. He knew his father (Richard) footsteps when he entered into the house. Richard wouldn't have to say a word when all of a sudden my baby would have the biggest and brightest smile on his face. My baby was also bound to a wheelchair. The doctor said the accident I was in caused my baby's condition. When I went unconscious, it cut off the oxygen from reaching his brains and damaged him. I was offered to put him in a rehabilitation house to reside in but I disapproved of someone else taking care of my baby. I would be concerned whether he would receive the proper care. I purchased a home so that he could have his own bedroom to store his physical impairment equipment that were allowable in the home. We lived in the home for 3 years before his passing away at the age of seven years old. I were in a daze. His passing just did not seem real to me. My grandmother Christine came to support me as usual and stayed with me until everything was over with and some over time. His passing was so painful but with God, he strengthen me. As time passed on through the years, God healed me. I thank God for giving us the strength and the ability to take care of our child from the beginning of his life to the end of his life. God brought us through.

Psalms 62:7 "In God is my salvation and my glory; the rock of my strength and my refuge is in God.

Nine years later prior to my youngest son death I lost my oldest son Martez at the age of eighteen to a senseless killing in the streets of Chicago – West Side. I and his father was in the present area at the time seeing him take his last breathe. The emotions and grieving that I and my family went through were unexplainable. This death was very hard on me; it was like my sons had taken a part of me along with them.

It took me years of healing but God kept me in the palm of his hands. I began to drink to ease the pain but my sorrow remained when I woke up the next day. My drinking went from a social drinker to a weekend drinker.

God is so good. I was surrounded by lots of partying because that's all I knew that would bring me some form of enjoyment. What I thought was fun at that time was not real fun. I didn't know Jesus but he knew me and he kept me and is still keeping me for his own purpose so that I would be able to testify about my life. He is an Awesome God. I had to go through the tests to have a testimony. God is a merciful God. He gets all the praises.

1 Peter 5:7 "Casting all my cares upon you for he cares for you".

As the years passed by, I begin to work several jobs and God slowly begin to heal my soul and strengthened me.

Philippian 4:13 "I can do all things through Christ which strengthened me."

I lost my sister Glender she and I were close and she would stay weekends with me. We enjoyed one another and we did many activities together. This happened a few years after my oldest son death but God will give you the strength you need in a time of need just ask him.

Matthew 7:7-8 (7) Ask, and it shall be given you. Seek and ye shall find, knock and it shall be opened unto you. (8) For everyone that asketh receiveth, and he that seeketh findeth, and to him that knocketh it shall be opened.

God called an angel in 2002, my grandmother Christine died. The one who will always come to support me and my family in a time of need as well as pleasant trips. By that time, I felt as if God were taking everyone who were closest to me and were for me, and celebrated me. Therefore, me and my entire family packed up our belongings and went to Mississippi to prepare for her funeral. I kept good memories in my heart for my grandmother. I felt good about our past. I have always showed my grandmother great hospitality throughout the years. She visited us whether it was a pleasant vacation or to support and do good deeds. My grandmother always will do good deeds.

I have always brought her nice gifts to show her how much I loved her, appreciated her, and taken her on outings like dining, to show her some parts of Chicago. She spread her love to all from childhood years to adults. My consciousness were clear of treating her kind.

My grandmother before her passing would always tell me if I wanted to see my sons again, I would have to get my life right with Christ. She was a strong believer and worked in the church faithfully. After her passing, I began to get a desire to go to church. I started watching church programs on T.V. not knowing at the time God was drawing me closer to him. God used my children to pull me in the church. All my children were saved until one day I was baptized and it was the best thing that ever happened to me. I was missing Jesus in my life. After I were baptized and accepted Jesus into my heart, God delivered me from 10years of smoking cigarettes and 15 years of drinking alcohol. The Bible says, Whom the Son sets free is free indeed. I am Free!

Psalms 107:20 - "He sent his Word and healed them (me) from their destruction.

2 Corinthians 5:17 – "Therefore, If any man be in Christ he is a new creature: Old things are passed away behold all things are become new.

In 2015, I lost my grandson Hughvon to the streets of Chicago. When my grandson passed, it was like a flashback from when my son was killed. I had to relive this tragedy all over again. My grandson left four children fatherless but through it all God is still good. He brought the family through these tragedies. I thank God because he will never leave you nor forsake you – Jesus Christ the same yesterday and today and forever – Hebrews 13:8

.

FAMILY GALLERY

NADINE & HUSBAND

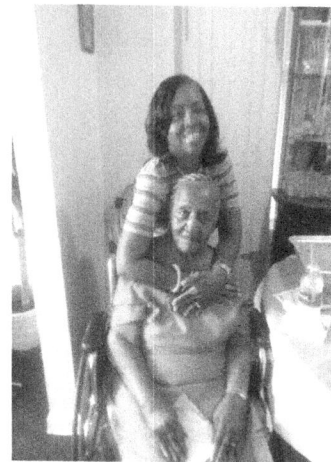

NADINE AND MOTHER

GRAND CHILDRENS

FAMILY GALLERY

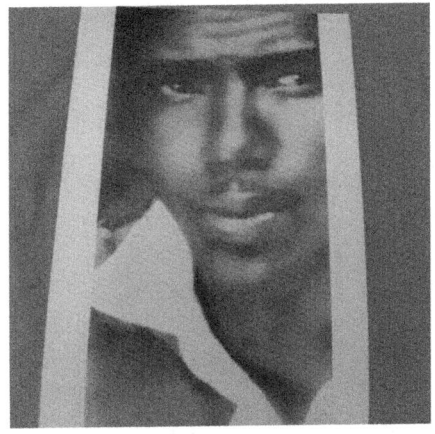

FATHER

NADINE

FAMILY GALLERY

SONS

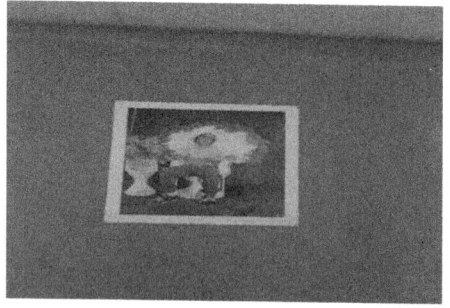

DAUGHTER

GRANDMOTHERS

ABOUT THE AUTHOR

My name is Nadine Bennett and I am the beautiful wife of Richard Bennett. We have been married for over 30 glorious years. We have three beautiful children, two boys (who are deceased - Martez and Terrance Lavelle), and a beautiful daughter Yolanda. I have five grandchildren and eight great grandchildren. I attended Wilbur Wright College where I obtained a Medical Office Certificate. I have several years of experience working in

the health field. I am also a licensed business owner in the food industry and I volunteer my time in the helps ministry at Living Word Christian Center. My passion is cooking soul food, traveling and exercising.

Now that you know a little about me let me tell you what my story is all about. This book is about my personal tragedies I encountered as a young girl growing into my womanhood. I remember my life took a turn when I lost my two sons and when I was in a car accident. These are just a few life events I survived through God's Grace and Mercy.

CONTACT INFORMATION

To purchase books by Nadine Bennett please send your request to:

Email Address:
Nadinebennett56@gmail.com

Phone Number:
773-266-2937

Website:
www.amazon.com

Publishing Company

A PASSAGE FOR MY BELOVED ONES

A passage for my entire beloved love one is who has transitioned from the earth into heaven. God makes no mistakes. All things happen for a reason. We may not see it nor understand but God knows all and sees all things. He does what is best for all, the family and the deceased he sees far more than we.

R.I.P. My Beloved Ones